Why Worrying is A Waste: A Biblical Perspective

Minister Jeremy B. Sims

Published by Jeremy Sims, 2023.

While every precaution has been taken in the preparation of this book, the publisher assumes no responsibility for errors or omissions, or for damages resulting from the use of the information contained herein.

WHY WORRYING IS A WASTE: A BIBLICAL PERSPECTIVE

First edition. October 6, 2023.

Copyright © 2023 Minister Jeremy B. Sims.

ISBN: 979-8223884507

Written by Minister Jeremy B. Sims.

Also by Minister Jeremy B. Sims

Stop Blaming the Adversary: It's You!
From Milk to Meat: The Journey of Spiritual Maturity
So You've Been Baptized, What's Next: The Road to Discipleship
Why Worrying is A Waste: A Biblical Perspective

Introduction: The Weight of Worry

You've been there, haven't you? Those nights when you find it hard to sleep, your mind racing with concerns about tomorrow, next week, next year. Worry has a sneaky way of creeping into our lives, doesn't it? But what if someone told you that your anxieties, while valid, are not serving your higher purpose? What if the Holy Scriptures, a book you hold dear, provides not just comfort, but a guide on how to transcend these worries?

This is not just any guide, but a divine one. The Bible, with its timeless wisdom, is rife with lessons on the futility of worry and the importance of trusting in a higher plan. By reflecting on these teachings, you will not only find peace but also a renewed purpose in your life's journey.

Why is worrying a waste? Well, in second person terms, because *you* are not meant to carry burdens that are too heavy for you. And this book aims to illustrate, enlighten, and inspire you to drop the weight of worry and embrace the light of trust.

The age-old scriptures provide multiple instances where individuals faced seemingly insurmountable challenges. But with trust in God's wisdom and purpose, they not only overcame but thrived. Your worries, big or small, are not unique in the grand tapestry of existence. And the good news is, there's a way out, a path illuminated by scripture.

Join us on this journey as we delve into why worrying is truly a waste, and how you can harness biblical teachings to find peace, purpose, and a profound trust in the journey that has been laid out for you.

Chapter 1. The Biblical Stance on Worry

Old Testament Teachings

THE OLD TESTAMENT, a foundational text for Christianity and many other religious traditions, offers insights about worry and trust. Here's what you can glean from its wisdom:

1. **God's Providence in Creation:**

"Look at the birds of the air: they neither sow nor reap nor gather into barns, and yet your heavenly Father feeds them. Are you not of more value than they?" (Proverbs 12:25)

This verse emphasizes that if God takes care of the birds, how much more will He care for you, His beloved creation? You are encouraged to recognize the divine providence in the natural world and to extrapolate it to your own life.

1. **Peace in God's Assurance:**

"When I am afraid, I put my trust in you." (Psalm 56:3)

Instead of succumbing to fear, the psalmist turns to trust in God. This serves as a reminder that in moments of doubt, anxiety, or fear, turning towards divine trust can alleviate worries.

1. **The Temporary Nature of Life's Troubles:**
    - *"Weeping may endure for a night, but joy comes in the morning."* (Psalm 30:5)
    - Worries and struggles are temporary, but God's love and blessings are eternal. This verse assures you that

even in your darkest moments, there's hope and light waiting.

New Testament Insights:

The New Testament further builds upon these teachings, emphasizing the message of Jesus and his apostles on the importance of casting aside worry.

1. **Jesus on Anxiety:**

"Therefore I tell you, do not worry about your life, what you will eat or drink; or about your body, what you will wear. Is not life more than food, and the body more than clothes?" (Matthew 6:25)

Jesus encourages believers to focus on the larger purpose of life rather than get bogged down by daily anxieties. He emphasizes the transient nature of material worries and underscores the lasting spiritual purpose.

1. **The Peace of God:**

"Do not be anxious about anything, but in every situation, by prayer and petition, with thanksgiving, present your requests to God. And the peace of God, which transcends all understanding, will guard your hearts and your minds in Christ Jesus." (Philippians 4:6-7)

This passage from Paul's letter to the Philippians stands as a powerful testament against worry. It encourages you to turn to prayer in moments of anxiety, assuring that God's peace will protect and guide you.

1. **Casting All Your Worries:**

"Cast all your anxiety on him because he cares for you." (1 Peter 5:7)

This verse reinforces the idea that God is a refuge. You're reminded that you don't need to bear your worries alone because God is willing and able to carry them for you.

———

THE SCRIPTURES, BOTH Old and New Testaments, converge on one profound truth: Worrying is not only futile but also detracts from the deeper, divine purpose of life. By understanding and internalizing these teachings, you can begin to move away from the bondage of worry towards a life rooted in trust and divine purpose.

Chapter 2: Worry Versus Trust: The Central Battle

———

LIFE OFTEN PRESENTS itself as a series of choices, and one of the most profound choices you grapple with is the choice between worry and trust. At its core, this decision underscores a deeper battle within: the need for control versus surrender to divine providence.

Trust in God's Plan:

1. **Understanding Divine Wisdom:**

One of the foundational tenets of the biblical narrative is that God, in His infinite wisdom, knows what is best for each of His creations. By this belief, even when the path is obscured with challenges and hurdles, it's leading you to a greater purpose.

"For I know the plans I have for you," declares the Lord, "plans to prosper you and not to harm you, plans to give you hope and a future." (Jeremiah 29:11)

This verse assures you that even in moments of uncertainty, God has a benevolent plan.

1. **Embracing The Unknown:**

While it's natural for you to want to know every detail of your journey, biblical teachings often underscore the importance of faith in the unseen.

"For we live by faith, not by sight." (2 Corinthians 5:7)

Here, you're reminded that true trust often requires embracing the unknown, trusting that the journey, even with its twists and turns, is divinely ordained.

1. **The Purpose Beyond Understanding**:

Often, the reasons for certain events or challenges might not be immediately clear. However, biblical teachings emphasize that there's a purpose beyond immediate comprehension.

"Trust in the Lord with all your heart and lean not on your own understanding; in all your ways submit to him, and he will make your paths straight." (Proverbs 3:5-6)

You're encouraged here to trust even when you don't understand, recognizing that divine understanding surpasses human reasoning.

Releasing Control:

1. **The Illusion of Control**:

Trying to control every aspect of life can be like trying to hold water in your hands; it's not only exhausting but also futile. The more you try to control, the more anxiety and worry seep in.

1. **Surrender as Strength**:

Contrary to popular belief, surrendering isn't a sign of weakness but rather a profound strength. By relinquishing the need to control, you make space for divine intervention and guidance.

"Come to me, all you who are weary and burdened, and I will give you rest." (Matthew 11:28)

Jesus extends an invitation to all who are burdened by life's anxieties to surrender and find rest in Him.

1. **Finding Freedom in Letting Go**:

Holding on to the reins of control might give a fleeting sense of security, but it's often accompanied by the constant dread of uncertainty. Releasing control, as counterintuitive as it might seem, can be the path to true freedom.

"The Spirit of the Lord is on me, because he has anointed me to proclaim good news to the poor. He has sent me to proclaim freedom for the prisoners and recovery of sight for the blind, to set the oppressed free." (Luke 4:18)

Through trust and surrender, you're promised freedom and clarity.

In conclusion, the central battle of worry versus trust is one that every believer encounters. By understanding the biblical emphasis on trusting in God's plan and releasing control, you can navigate life with a heart anchored in faith and a spirit unburdened by needless worry.

Chapter 3: The Physical, Emotional, and Spiritual Consequences of Worry

———

WORRY, WHILE OFTEN considered a natural part of the human experience, carries profound consequences that touch every aspect of your being. From the stories and teachings of the Bible to contemporary research, it's evident that excessive worry has tangible effects on your physical, emotional, and spiritual well-being.

1. Physical Consequences:

Fatigue: Constant worry and anxiety can drain your energy, leading to persistent fatigue and tiredness. Just as Moses was weary leading the Israelites, excessive worry can make you feel as if you're wandering in a desert of fatigue.

Sleep Disturbances: Remember the stories of King Saul who was tormented and couldn't find rest? Chronic worry can lead to sleep disturbances, insomnia, and restless nights.

Weakened Immune System: Just as the body of the Israelites was vulnerable in the wilderness, constant stress and worry can weaken your immune system, making you more susceptible to infections.

Digestive Issues: Worry can manifest in physical symptoms like stomach aches, indigestion, or even more severe digestive problems.

2. Emotional Consequences:

Decreased Ability to Cope: Just as the waters of Meribah were bitter, excessive worry can make life's challenges seem insurmountable, decreasing your resilience and ability to cope with adversity.

Impaired Decision Making: When Solomon asked God for wisdom, he was seeking clarity. Worry, on the other hand, clouds judgment and hampers decision-making abilities.

Decreased Enjoyment in Life: Like David in his times of distress, you might find it hard to find joy and satisfaction in life's blessings when overshadowed by constant worry.

Strained Relationships: Worry can strain relationships, as seen in the conflicts among the disciples. When you're constantly anxious, it can lead to irritability and tension with loved ones.

3. Spiritual Consequences:

Diminished Faith: Just as Peter began to sink when he took his eyes off Jesus and focused on the storm, worry can divert your focus from God and diminish your faith.

Barrier in Relationship with God: Like the walls of Jericho that kept the Israelites out, unchecked worry can become a barrier, preventing a close relationship with God.

Lost Opportunities for Witness: Instead of being a beacon of hope and faith, when you're consumed with worry, it becomes challenging to witness and share God's goodness effectively.

Reduced Prayer Life: Instead of turning to God in prayer, constant worry might make you feel distant or even resentful, reducing the quality of your prayer life.

The Bible tells us in Philippians 4:6-7, *"Do not be anxious about anything, but in every situation, by prayer and petition, with thanksgiving, present your requests to God. And the peace of God, which transcends all understanding, will guard your hearts and your minds in Christ Jesus."* This is a profound reminder of the alternative to worry: turning to God, surrendering concerns, and embracing the peace that surpasses understanding.

———

IN CONCLUSION, WHILE it might seem natural or even justifiable to worry, it's crucial to recognize the multi-dimensional consequences of unchecked anxiety. Through biblical wisdom and trust in divine providence, you can navigate life's challenges without the heavy burdens that worry brings.

Chapter 4: Stories of Trust: Biblical Examples of Faith Amidst Uncertainty

THROUGHOUT THE SCRIPTURES, countless individuals exhibited profound trust in God, even when faced with overwhelming uncertainties. Their stories not only serve as testimonies of their faith but also as inspiration for you to navigate your own life's challenges.

1. Abraham's Leap of Faith:

The Call and Promise: When God called Abraham (then Abram) to leave his homeland and go to a land that He would show him, Abraham obeyed without knowing the final destination (Genesis 12:1-4). This was a massive leap of faith as he left behind familiar territory, trusted God's promise, and embarked on an unknown journey.

The Ultimate Test: Probably the most profound test of Abraham's faith was when God asked him to sacrifice his son, Isaac (Genesis 22:1-19). Even in this heart-wrenching situation, Abraham's trust did not waver. He believed in God's promise, and his willingness to obey showcased his unyielding faith. In the end, God provided a ram as a substitute for Isaac, reiterating His promise and faithfulness.

Takeaway: Abraham's story exemplifies that sometimes God's plans may seem incomprehensible or even contradictory. Yet, trusting in His greater purpose can lead to blessings beyond understanding.

2. Job's Unwavering Trust:

The Calamities: Job, a man described as blameless and upright, faced severe trials. He lost his children, his wealth, and was afflicted with painful sores (Job 1-2). Despite these overwhelming adversities, Job did not curse God.

Struggling with Despair: Though Job lamented his miseries and sought answers for his sufferings, his foundation of faith was unshaken. Even when his wife told him to curse God and die, Job replied, *"Shall we accept good from God, and not trouble?"* (Job 2:10).

Restoration and Reward: In the end, God not only restored Job's fortunes but also blessed him abundantly for his unwavering faith (Job 42:10-17).

Takeaway: Job's story teaches that even in extreme suffering and loss, remaining steadfast in faith and seeking God can lead to restoration and blessings.

3. Jesus in the Garden of Gethsemane:

The Agony of Anticipation: On the night before His crucifixion, Jesus went to the Garden of Gethsemane to pray (Matthew 26:36-46). He was deeply distressed, knowing the agony that awaited Him. In His humanity, Jesus expressed his dread, *"My soul is overwhelmed with sorrow to the point of death."*

Surrendering to the Divine Will: Despite His anguish, Jesus's prayer was one of profound trust and surrender. He prayed, *"My Father, if it is possible, may this cup be taken from me. Yet not as I will, but as you will."* This utterance is a profound reflection of Jesus's trust in God's plan.

Takeaway: Jesus's time in Gethsemane demonstrates that it's natural to feel overwhelmed or fearful of upcoming challenges. However, the ultimate act of trust is surrendering to God's will and believing in His overarching plan for good.

Each of these biblical figures faced immense uncertainties and challenges. Yet, their stories illuminate the path of trust, showing that even in the midst of profound struggles, placing unwavering faith in God leads to divine guidance, blessings, and ultimately, a deeper relationship with the Creator

Chapter 5: Strategies to Overcome Worry

IN THE INTRICATE FABRIC of life, it's only natural for you to encounter moments of anxiety and worry. However, succumbing to these feelings can be debilitating. By turning to time-tested strategies, both biblical and contemporary, you can find solace, grounding, and even transformation amidst the chaos of concern.

1. Prayer and Reflection:

Direct Communication with the Divine:

Just as King David poured out his fears and worries to God in the Psalms, prayer offers you a direct line of communication with the Divine. In moments of anxiety, turning your concerns into prayers can be a transformative act.

Meditative Reflection:

Setting aside quiet moments for reflection can provide clarity amidst chaos. Reflecting on God's promises, recalling past instances of His faithfulness, or simply contemplating His attributes can be a source of comfort.

SCRIPTURE MEDITATION:

Immersing yourself in scripture provides both wisdom and encouragement. Verses like Philippians 4:6-7 remind you not to be anxious and to present your requests to God, assuring that His peace will guard your heart and mind.

Guided Prayers:

If you find it challenging to articulate your anxieties, turning to guided prayers or existing Psalms can be a way to resonate with feelings penned down centuries ago but are still relevant today.

2. Embracing the Present:

Mindfulness and Grounding:

Being present means being fully engaged in the current moment, setting aside regrets of the past or anxieties about the future. Simple grounding exercises, like focusing on your breath or engaging your senses (what you hear, see, touch, taste, or smell), can divert attention from spiraling worries and anchor you to the present.

Gratitude Journaling:

Cultivating a habit of noting down things you're grateful for can shift your focus from what's lacking or uncertain to what's abundant and certain in your life. Just as the Israelites recounted God's blessings during their journeys, you too can find solace in recognizing everyday blessings.

Active Engagement:

Engaging in activities that you love and are passionate about can act as a distraction from overwhelming thoughts. Be it gardening, reading, or any other hobby, immersing yourself can serve as a reminder to enjoy the current moment.

Nature Walks:

Spending time in nature, observing the lilies of the field and the birds of the air, as Jesus mentioned in Matthew 6:25-34, can be a poignant reminder that if God takes care of the natural world, how much more will He care for you? Recognizing the beauty and rhythm of nature can act as a balm for anxious thoughts and help you embrace the present.

IN CONCLUSION:

While it's natural to experience worry, it doesn't have to define or control your life. By integrating strategies such as prayer and reflection and embracing the present moment, you not only combat these feelings but also cultivate a deeper sense of peace and purpose. These methods, rooted in both biblical wisdom and contemporary practices, can guide you in navigating life's uncertainties with faith and resilience. Remember the words from 1 Peter 5:7, *"Cast all your anxiety on him because he cares for you."* This profound truth serves as a reminder that you're never alone in your struggles and that there's a divine source of strength available to you at all times.

Chapter 6: The Power of Surrender and Contentment

SURRENDER AND CONTENTMENT are potent spiritual principles found throughout history and revered in biblical teachings. When woven into the fabric of everyday life, these principles offer profound shifts in perception, resilience, and overall well-being. Let's delve deeper into the transformative power of surrender and contentment, especially in the context of biblical teachings, to understand how they can reshape your life journey.

1. The Principle of Surrender:

Biblical Context: The concept of surrender permeates the scriptures. Jesus's words, *"Not my will, but yours be done,"* (Luke 22:42) in the Garden of Gethsemane epitomize the ultimate act of surrender. By entrusting His life and purpose to God's plan, Jesus exemplified complete surrender.

Relinquishing Control: In life, striving to control every aspect often leads to stress and exhaustion. By surrendering, you recognize that not everything is within your hands. This doesn't mean inaction but rather co-partnering with God, taking action, and then releasing the outcome.

Freedom in Letting Go: Surrender is about freedom. When you surrender, you free yourself from the bondage of expectations, fears, and the need to control, opening up a space for God's will to unfold.

2. The Principle of Contentment:

Biblical Context: Paul's words in Philippians 4:11-12, *"I have learned to be content whatever the circumstances,"* highlight contentment as a learned and cultivated virtue. Paul acknowledges both abundance and need, emphasizing that contentment isn't based on external conditions but internal perspective.

Finding Joy in the Present: Instead of constantly yearning for more or dwelling on what's missing, contentment focuses on finding joy and gratitude in the present. It resonates with Jesus's teachings on considering the lilies and birds, emphasizing God's provision (Matthew 6:25-34).

An Antidote to Consumerism: In a society driven by consumerism and the constant chase for more, contentment is a counter-cultural stance. It is an invitation to appreciate the value of what you have and find richness in simplicity.

The Confluence of Surrender and Contentment:

Peace Amidst Storms: Both surrender and contentment anchor you in a state of peace. By surrendering control and being content in the present, you cultivate a steadiness of heart, even amidst life's storms.

Deepening Trust: Surrender is an act of trust, trusting that God's plan is supreme. Contentment complements this by fostering trust that what you have now, and where you are, holds purpose and value.

Spiritual Growth: These principles aren't just passive states; they're catalysts for spiritual growth. In the process of surrendering and finding contentment, you draw closer to God, deepening your relationship and understanding of His character and promises.

CONCLUSION:

Embracing surrender and contentment isn't about passive resignation but an empowered choice. It's about recognizing God's omnipresence in your life, believing in His promises, and finding joy and gratitude in the present moment. These principles, deeply rooted in biblical teachings, provide a roadmap to navigate life with grace, trust, and a heart anchored in peace.

Conclusion: Living a Life Free from the Chains of Worry

The journey through life is filled with highs and lows, joys and sorrows, certainties and ambiguities. While it's natural for worry to emerge as a companion on this journey, it need not dictate the rhythm of your steps. As you've discovered through the biblical lens, the antidote to worry lies in understanding and internalizing principles like surrender, trust, and contentment.

To live free from the chains of worry is not to deny or avoid challenges but to approach them with a changed perspective. It's about realizing that worry, at its core, is a reflection of trying to control the uncontrollable. But when you surrender control, trust in the divine plan, and find contentment in the present, the weight of worry lightens.

Recall the age-old wisdom found in the Sermon on the Mount, where Jesus beckons, *"Do not worry about tomorrow, for tomorrow will worry about itself. Each day has enough trouble of its own"* (Matthew 6:34). Here lies a profound truth: by embracing the present moment and entrusting the future to God, you liberate yourself from the mental burdens that often overshadow the beauty of the 'now'.

Living free from worry also paves the way for a deeper spiritual connection. It allows for a more intimate relationship with God, fostering a trust built on experiences of His faithfulness. As the apostle Peter encourages, *"Cast all your anxiety on Him because He cares for you"* (1 Peter 5:7), you're reminded that you are not alone in your battles or burdens.

Moreover, this freedom brings about a ripple effect. As you navigate life with a heart unburdened by excessive worry, you become a beacon of hope and resilience for others. Your journey becomes a testament to the transformative power of faith, trust, and contentment.

In essence, life free from the chains of worry is not a life free from challenges but one where challenges are met with grace, trust, and an unwavering faith in God's sovereignty. It's a life where each day is embraced as a gift, with its mysteries and marvels, and where the future, no matter how uncertain, is viewed with hope and anticipation.

May you walk this journey with a heart lightened by trust, eyes that see beyond the immediate, and a spirit anchored in the unchanging love and promises of God.

Let's Dive a Little Deeper Breaking the Chains: Understanding the Futility of Worry Through a Biblical Lens"

Introduction

WORRY. IT'S A FEELING that you, like countless others, are all too familiar with. It's a constant background noise, an ever-present companion in today's fast-paced world. But what if you paused for a moment and asked: Why do you worry? And is it truly beneficial? This exploration will journey through the biblical landscape to unravel the deep-seated nature of worry and the liberating alternative that God offers you.

The Origin of Worry

Before you can tackle the issue of worry, it's essential to understand its origins. In the Bible, the first instance of fear and hiding appears immediately after the fall of man. Adam and Eve, after committing sin, felt fear and hid from God. This emotional reaction demonstrates that worry and fear have deep roots, often tied to a sense of inadequacy or guilt.

Worry is as ancient as humanity itself. From a biblical perspective, the genesis of worry can be traced back to the Garden of Eden. After Adam and Eve partook of the forbidden fruit, they felt fear for the first time, hiding from God's presence. This feeling was birthed from the awareness of their inadequacy, guilt, and the consequences of their actions.

From a psychological viewpoint, worry is a natural response to potential threats. Evolutionarily, early humans needed this alert system to survive in a world filled with real and immediate dangers. However, in today's modern world, the lines have blurred between actual threats and perceived ones, leading to chronic worry for many.

Perspective on Worry's Origin:

Understanding the root of worry is essential for managing it. When you know that at the core of worry often lies a fear of the unknown, loss of control, or potential negative outcomes, it becomes evident that:

1. **Worry is Natural**: It's a common human emotion, designed to keep you safe. However, chronic worry is a distortion of this protective mechanism.
2. **Worry is Rooted in Uncertainty**: Adam and Eve worried because they did not know the full ramifications of their actions. Similarly, you worry when you can't predict or control future outcomes.

3. **Faith & Trust are Antidotes**: The Bible consistently presents faith, trust, and surrender to God's plan as remedies for worry. This implies that understanding and strengthening one's faith can be a potent antidote to chronic worry.

CHECKLIST: TACKLING the Roots of Worry

1. **Self-awareness**: Regularly check in with yourself. Understand what triggers your worry. Is it a genuine concern or an imagined scenario?
2. **Limit Exposure**: If watching the news or certain activities increase your anxiety, limit your exposure. Stay informed but don't inundate yourself.
3. **Scripture Meditation**: Delve into scriptures that address worry and fear. Verses like Philippians 4:6-7 and Matthew 6:34 can offer comfort.
4. **Pray Regularly**: Communicate with God about your fears and worries. Remember 1 Peter 5:7: *"Cast all your anxiety on him because he cares for you."*
5. **Stay Present**: Practice mindfulness and meditation to stay rooted in the present.
6. **Seek Counsel**: If worry becomes overwhelming, don't hesitate to seek counsel, whether from a trusted spiritual leader or a mental health professional.
7. **Focus on Action**: Determine if there's any actionable step you can take to address the cause of your worry. If not, practice surrendering it.
8. **Practice Gratitude**: Daily jot down things you're grateful for. Gratitude shifts your focus from what might go wrong to what's going right.

9. **Engage in Physical Activity**: Exercise is a known stress-reliever. Even a short walk can clear your mind.
10. **Limit Stimulants**: Reduce intake of caffeine or other stimulants that might heighten anxiety.
11. **Stay Connected**: Talk to loved ones. Sharing worries can often reduce their weight.

In understanding the origin and perspective of worry, and armed with a practical checklist, you can navigate the complexities of life with a renewed sense of purpose, faith, and resilience. The journey might not always be free of worry, but with the right tools and mindset, you can ensure it doesn't dominate your narrative.

The Illusion of Control

The heart of worry often lies in a desire for control. You worry because you want to be certain, to ensure that everything goes according to plan. But remember the Tower of Babel? Humanity tried to build a tower to the heavens, to make a name for themselves. They sought control, but God, in His infinite wisdom, scattered them. You're reminded that no matter how hard you try, some things are beyond your grasp.

The concept of control is deeply ingrained in the human psyche. As people, you naturally want to believe that you have agency over your life's events. Yet, the Bible and countless lived experiences tell a different story. Consider the Tower of Babel, where humanity tried to reach the heavens. They believed they were in control, yet were humbled by God's intervention. This story, among others, highlights a recurring theme: the limited scope of human control juxtaposed against divine or unforeseen forces.

Perspective on the Illusion of Control:

God's Sovereignty: In religious terms, the essence of many biblical teachings is recognizing God's sovereignty over all things. In Proverbs 19:21, it's said: *"Many are the plans in a person's heart, but it is the Lord's purpose that prevails."* This perspective teaches surrender and humility.

Existential Reality: Even outside religious texts, life itself often demonstrates the fragility of human control. Whether it's unexpected weather changes, health issues, or global events, unpredictability is a fundamental aspect of existence.

Control vs. Effort: There's a distinct difference between effort and control. While you can control your actions, efforts, and responses, the outcomes often lie beyond your grasp.

Checklist: Navigating the Illusion of Control

1. **Acceptance**: Regularly remind yourself that not everything is within your control. Acceptance is the first step towards peace.

1. **Mindful Meditation**: Engage in practices that encourage being in the present moment, as they highlight the power of now over future uncertainties.
2. **Reflect on Past Experiences**: Remember times when unexpected events turned out beneficial or when your plans didn't work, but things still turned out okay.
3. **Seek Guidance in Scripture**: Delve into biblical stories of those who showed faith even when control was out of their hands.
4. **Set Realistic Expectations**: It's essential to set achievable goals. Remember, you can control your efforts, not the outcomes.
5. **Focus on Response**: While you can't control every situation, you can control your response to it. Developing resilience and adaptability is key.

6. **Avoid Overplanning**: While planning is crucial, it's equally important not to become rigid. Leave room for spontaneity and unpredictability.

7. **Prayer and Surrender**: Regularly communicate with God, handing over your anxieties and seeking guidance.

8. **Stay Connected**: Share your feelings of uncertainty with loved ones or support groups. They can offer a different perspective and reassurance.

9. **Limit Overconsumption of Information**: In the age of the internet, the influx of information can be overwhelming and can create an illusion of control. Consume wisely.

10. **Celebrate Small Wins**: Focus on and celebrate small achievements, acknowledging the efforts you've put in, regardless of the outcome.

Understanding and coming to terms with the illusion of control can be liberating. It teaches you humility, the value of surrender, and the importance of faith. While you play your part in the grand scheme of life, recognizing the vastness of the universe and the divine plan allows you to navigate life with a balanced perspective, ensuring that when things don't go as planned, you remain anchored in faith and understanding.

The Biblical Perspective on Tomorrow

Jesus, in His sermon on the mount, addressed worry head-on. *"Do not worry about tomorrow, for tomorrow will worry about itself."* (Matthew 6:34) Why did He emphasize this? This chapter will delve deep into the profound wisdom behind these words and how it can transform your perspective on the future.

Throughout the Bible, the theme of tomorrow resonates with teachings about faith, trust, and the transcendence of divine will over human planning. Jesus's proclamation, *"Therefore do not worry about tomorrow, for tomorrow will worry about itself. Each day has enough trouble of its own"* (Matthew 6:34), captures the essence of this perspective. The emphasis here isn't on neglecting preparation but on avoiding undue anxiety and understanding the limited scope of human foresight.

PERSPECTIVE ON TOMORROW from a Biblical Viewpoint:

Emphasis on Today: While the Bible doesn't discourage planning or being future-oriented, it cautions against excessive worry about the future, urging focus on the present.

Trust in Divine Providence: The underlying sentiment in the biblical teachings about tomorrow is trusting in God's provision and guidance.

Transient Nature of Life: Biblical teachings often highlight the fleeting nature of life. James 4:14 states: *"You do not even know what will happen tomorrow. What is your life? You are a mist that appears for a little while and then vanishes."* This sentiment underscores the significance of living in the present.

Checklist: Embracing the Biblical Perspective on Tomorrow

1. **Daily Reflection**: Start or end your day by reflecting on the blessings and lessons of the present day.

2. **Limit Future-focused Anxiety**: Differentiate between productive planning and excessive worrying. Take steps towards your goals, but release attachment to specific outcomes.

3. **Pray for Guidance**: Seek God's guidance for the future through prayer, asking for wisdom and clarity.

4. **Dive into Scripture**: Study Bible verses that emphasize the importance of the present, such as Proverbs 27:1: *"Do not boast about tomorrow, for you do not know what a day may bring."*

5. **Cultivate Contentment**: Regularly practice gratitude for the present, cherishing the current moments and blessings.

6. **Engage in Present-focused Activities**: Activities like gardening, painting, or playing an instrument can help anchor you in the present.

7. **Limit Exposure to Anxiety-inducing Media**: Constantly consuming media about potential future threats can amplify anxiety. Stay informed, but balance it with uplifting content.

8. **Seek Community**: Sharing your hopes and concerns about the future within a trusted community or support group can offer reassurance and guidance.

9. **Embrace Flexibility**: While it's valuable to have plans, remain open to the idea that God's plan might differ and be even better.

10. **Set Aside Worry Time**: If you find it challenging to manage worry, allocate a specific short time daily for it. When that time is up, consciously move on to another activity.

11. **Celebrate Small Daily Achievements**: Instead of solely focusing on long-term goals, find joy in the little

accomplishments each day offers.

EMBRACING THE BIBLICAL perspective on tomorrow doesn't mean forsaking preparation or foresight. It means balancing preparedness with trust, recognizing the divine's role in shaping tomorrow, and finding peace in today. By incorporating these insights and tools into your life, you're not just reducing anxiety but aligning closer with a faith that assures God's providence in every tomorrow.

Worry and Your Relationship with God

When you worry, you're not just expressing concern about the future; you might also be reflecting your relationship with God. Do you trust Him? The Israelites, despite witnessing miracles, worried about food and water in the wilderness. Their worry was a reflection of their faith. How does your worry mirror your faith?

At its core, worry is a manifestation of fear, uncertainty, and a perceived lack of control. It can often signify a deep-seated struggle to trust fully in God's sovereignty. The Bible speaks of worry in various contexts, emphasizing that it can be a barrier to an intimate relationship with God. Jesus said, *"Can any one of you by worrying add a single hour to your life?"* (Matthew 6:27) suggesting that worrying is not only futile but might also be a sign of misplaced priorities.

Perspective on Worry in Relation to God:

Worry as a Lack of Trust: In biblical terms, incessant worrying can signify a wavering trust in God's promises. The Bible assures, *"And we know that in all things God works for the good of those who love him, who have been called according to his purpose."* (Romans 8:28)

Worry Diverts Focus: Chronic worry can shift focus from God's omnipotence to one's own inadequacies or the vastness of a problem.

God as the Ultimate Provider: The Bible consistently reinforces the idea of God as a provider. Jesus used the example of birds, which don't sow or reap, yet are fed by their Heavenly Father, to illustrate this (Matthew 6:26).

Checklist: Strengthening Your Relationship with God Amidst Worry

1. **Daily Prayer**: Intentionally set aside time each day to communicate your worries to God, surrendering them and seeking His peace.
2. **Scripture Immersion**: Dive deep into Bible verses that address worry, fear, and trust. Philippians 4:6-7 and Psalm 55:22 can be comforting starting points.
3. **Christian Meditation**: Meditate on God's attributes. Reflecting on His omnipotence, love, and sovereignty can reframe your perspective on worries.
4. **Journaling**: Document your worries and over time, note down how situations unfold. Often, you'll see patterns of worries unfounded and God's subtle interventions.
5. **Seek Spiritual Guidance**: Engage in discussions with spiritual leaders or mentors about your anxieties. They can offer insights, prayers, and support.

1. **Join a Community**: Participate in a faith-based group where you can share and listen to others' experiences. This can give a collective sense of God's work in lives.
2. **Serve Others**: By focusing on serving others, you can often gain perspective on your worries and experience firsthand God's providence.
3. **Practice Gratitude**: Daily acknowledge blessings, big and small. This redirects focus from what might go wrong to evidence of God's ongoing presence in your life.
4. **Embrace Worship**: Participate in worship sessions, whether in church or at home. Songs and hymns can uplift spirits and realign focus.
5. **Trust in God's Timing**: Remember that God's timing is

impeccable, even if it doesn't align with yours. Recalling past instances where His timing proved perfect can reinforce trust.

---

1. **Seek Balance**: While it's essential to trust God, it's equally vital to take actionable steps where you can, acknowledging that faith and action often go hand-in-hand.

WHEN WORRY SEEMS OVERWHELMING, remember that it's a signal, an invitation to lean more into your relationship with God. It's an opportunity to deepen your faith, realign your focus, and experience the profound peace that comes from unwavering trust in Him. By incorporating these insights and tools into your life, not only will the grip of worry lessen, but your spiritual journey will be enriched.

The Futility of Worry

Solomon, in all his wisdom, remarked, *"Who of you by worrying can add a single hour to your life?"* (Luke 12:25). Worry doesn't change outcomes. This chapter will dissect this profound statement and showcase the sheer futility of worry through biblical narratives and teachings.

Worry is a universal experience, but its tangible benefits are hard to identify. Instead, it often brings anxiety, sleeplessness, and stress, affecting physical and mental health. As the Bible eloquently states in Matthew 6:27, *"Which of you by worrying can add a single hour to his lifespan?"* This introspective question underscores the heart of worry's ineffectiveness.

Perspective on the Futility of Worry:

Misplaced Energy: Worry consumes energy that could be channeled into productive tasks or positive thinking, making it an inefficient allocation of mental resources.

Cyclical Trap: Worry tends to be self-perpetuating. The more you worry, the more you fixate on potential negative outcomes, which in turn amplifies the worry.

Distorted Reality: Chronic worry can skew perception, leading you to focus predominantly on worst-case scenarios, which might never materialize.

CHECKLIST: REDIRECTING the Energy Spent on Worry

1. **Awareness**: Recognize and label your feelings. Simply acknowledging "I am worrying" can sometimes reduce the emotion's intensity.
2. **Limit 'Worry Time'**: Allocate a specific, short period each day for worrying. When time's up, consciously redirect your attention elsewhere.
3. **Focus on Actionable Concerns**: Divide your worries into actionable and non-actionable concerns. Address the actionable worries by creating a plan or taking small steps towards a solution.
4. **Mindfulness and Meditation**: Ground yourself in the present moment. Techniques like deep breathing, meditation, or even simple mindfulness exercises can break the cycle of chronic worry.
5. **Stay Connected**: Talk to someone you trust about your concerns. Sometimes, verbalizing worries can put them in perspective.
6. **Engage in Physical Activity**: Physical exercise can act as an

outlet for nervous energy and release endorphins, reducing stress.

7. **Limit Media Consumption**: Constant exposure to negative news can fuel worries. Stay informed but set boundaries on your media intake.

8. **Challenge Negative Thoughts**: When a worrisome thought enters your mind, challenge it. Ask yourself: Is it true? Is it the worst-case scenario? Is there a positive angle?

9. **Focus on Gratitude**: Each day, list three things you're grateful for. This habit can shift focus from what's lacking or uncertain to what's abundant in your life.

10. **Seek Professional Help**: If worry becomes overwhelming, consider seeking help from a therapist or counselor trained in cognitive-behavioral therapy or anxiety management.

1. **Remember Past Triumphs**: Remind yourself of past worries that never materialized or times when you overcame challenges. This can reinforce the understanding of worry's often baseless nature.

Understanding the futility of worry is the first step towards managing it. By adopting a proactive approach, grounded in the realities of today and not the uncertainties of tomorrow, you can reclaim the mental energy that worry consumes and channel it into more fruitful pursuits, creating a healthier and more balanced life.

Trust – The Antidote to Worry

Throughout the Bible, trust stands tall as the antidote to worry. From Abraham's trust in God's promise of progeny to David's trust as he faced Goliath, you'll explore how trust has been the bedrock of faith and the solution to worry.

Worry often arises from feelings of uncertainty, vulnerability, or perceived threats. At its heart, trust is the profound belief in the reliability, ability, or strength of someone or something. In spiritual contexts, trust in a higher power, such as God, is presented as the ultimate antidote to worry. Psalm 56:3 says, *"When I am afraid, I put my trust in you."* This affirmation beautifully showcases how trust can counteract the debilitating effects of worry.

Perspective on Trust as the Solution to Worry:

Trust Transcends Understanding: Trusting, especially in divine providence, doesn't always require understanding the bigger picture. It's a heartfelt surrender.

Foundation of Faith: Trust is the cornerstone of faith. Faith isn't merely believing that God exists, but trusting Him in all circumstances.

Releasing Control: Recognizing that we don't have control over every aspect of life, and putting trust in a higher power or the process, alleviates the need to worry.

Checklist: Cultivating Trust to Alleviate Worry

1. **Daily Devotion**: Dedicate a specific time for spiritual practice, be it prayer, meditation, or scripture reading. This daily connection fosters trust.
2. **Journaling**: Maintain a trust journal, documenting moments

when trust overcame worry or when perceived worries were unfounded.

3. **Affirmations**: Repeat affirmations that reinforce trust, such as *"I trust the process,"* or *"I trust in God's plan for me."*

4. **Seek Support**: Surround yourself with trust-oriented individuals, whether they be mentors, faith leaders, or supportive friends and family.

5. **Reflect on Past Experiences**: Recall moments in life when trust guided you through difficult times, reinforcing its potency as an antidote to worry.

6. **Engage in Trust-building Activities**: Engage in activities that naturally build trust, such as team-building exercises or trust falls.

7. **Study Trustworthy Figures**: Dive into stories or biographies of individuals who exemplified trust in their lives, drawing inspiration from their experiences.

8. **Avoid Overanalyzing**: Sometimes, the more we analyze, the more we worry. Trust often requires taking a step back and letting things unfold.

9. **Visualize Positive Outcomes**: Instead of envisioning worst-case scenarios, actively visualize positive outcomes and trust in their potential manifestation.

10. **Prayer and Meditation**: Cultivate a routine of prayer or meditation focusing on surrender and trust. Hand over your worries and trust in the guidance received.

11. **Practice Patience**: Trust is often about waiting patiently. Develop patience through practices like deep breathing when impatience strikes.

Trust, in its essence, is the release of the incessant need for control. It's the understanding that there's a bigger plan, one that might not always be evident. By actively choosing trust over worry, you not only find peace in the present moment but also align with a force much greater than individual concerns. This alignment paves the way for serenity, even in the face of life's unpredictable storms.

Embracing God's Sovereignty

Understanding God's sovereignty is crucial. It's about acknowledging that God's plan and wisdom surpass human understanding. By exploring the stories of Job, Esther, and Joseph, you'll witness how God's overarching sovereignty transformed tragedies into triumphs.

God's sovereignty refers to His ultimate power, authority, and all-encompassing control over the events of the universe. Understanding this aspect of God's nature provides a deep sense of security for believers. Romans 8:28 states, *"And we know that in all things God works for the good of those who love him, who have been called according to his purpose."* Embracing this sovereignty means believing that even in the midst of turbulence, God's hand is guiding, shaping, and leading towards a greater purpose.

Perspective on God's Sovereignty:

The Infinite Canvas: God's viewpoint is beyond human comprehension. He sees the entirety of time and space, orchestrating events for a grander plan.

> **Beyond Human Control**: Recognizing our limitations in understanding or controlling every event, and accepting that God's plans are greater than ours, can be a liberating realization.

> **Assurance in Unpredictability**: Embracing God's sovereignty means finding peace amidst life's unpredictability, knowing that He is in control.

Checklist: Embracing the Sovereignty of God in Daily Life

1. **Study Scriptures**: Delve into biblical passages that emphasize

God's sovereignty, such as Psalms 115:3, Proverbs 19:21, and Isaiah 46:10.

2. **Meditative Prayer**: Spend moments in prayer focusing solely on the acknowledgment of God's grandeur and control over all creation.

3. **Contemplate Nature**: Observing the wonders of nature can be a gentle reminder of the Creator's intricate designs and mastery.

1. **Engage in Worship**: Joining collective worship sessions can be a way to corporately acknowledge and celebrate God's sovereignty.

2. **Seek Theological Understanding**: If doubts arise, consider theological studies or discussions that focus on the doctrine of God's sovereignty.

3. **Share Testimonies**: Sharing personal stories of times when God's hand was evident can bolster your faith and that of others.

4. **Acceptance in Prayer**: Instead of always presenting requests, have prayers of pure acceptance, embracing whatever God has in store.

5. **Limit Human Dependency**: While it's natural to seek guidance from others, ensure your ultimate trust remains in God's sovereign will.

6. **Affirm God's Control**: When faced with decisions or uncertainties, mentally (or verbally) affirm that God's will shall prevail.

1. **Journaling**: Document instances when unforeseen events turned out for your good or revealed a greater purpose, recognizing God's sovereign hand in them.

2. **Counsel and Guidance**: If struggling with accepting God's control, consider spiritual counseling or joining faith-based

groups centered on this topic.

Embracing God's sovereignty does not mean passivity or relinquishing personal responsibility. Instead, it means aligning oneself with the belief that there's a divine orchestration in the universe, a dance of events choreographed by the greatest Maestro. It's about surrendering the need to always understand, and instead choosing to trust and rest in the assurance of God's infinite wisdom and boundless love.

PRACTICAL STEPS: FROM Worry to Peace

How can you, in your everyday life, transition from a state of constant worry to one of peace? From the practice of daily prayer to immersing oneself in scriptures and seeking Godly counsel, this chapter will offer you tangible steps, grounded in biblical teachings, to attain that coveted peace.

Life's unpredictability often triggers worry, an emotion rooted in uncertainty, fear, and anxiety about the future. Yet, despite its prevalence, worry rarely offers any tangible benefits. On the contrary, it drains emotional energy and magnifies problems. Peace, in stark contrast, offers serenity, clarity, and a stable mindset. Isaiah 26:3 declares, *"You will keep in perfect peace those whose minds are steadfast, because they trust in you."* This transition from worry to peace is more than possible; it's a journey deeply rooted in faith and trust.

Perspective on the Shift from Worry to Peace:

Inherent Inefficiency of Worry: Recognize that worry does not change outcomes; it only alters your mental state and can hinder effective problem-solving.

Peace as a Choice: Understand that peace isn't merely the absence of conflict but a conscious decision to remain calm amidst the storm.

Faith as the Bridge: Faith acts as the bridge between worry and peace. It offers a perspective that transcends the immediacy of issues and anchors the soul in divine assurance.

Practical Checklist: Transitioning from Worry to Peace

1. **Identify the Root**: Before addressing worry, identify its root cause. Ask yourself, "What specifically am I worried about?"
2. **Scriptural Meditation**: Focus on scriptures that emphasize peace and God's providence, such as Philippians 4:6-7 and John 14:27.

1. **Active Surrender**: Actively hand over your worries to God in prayer. Imagine placing them at His feet and walking away lighter.
2. **Mindful Breathing**: Use deep breathing exercises to calm the mind and anchor yourself in the present moment.
3. **Limit Information Intake**: Overexposure to negative news or excessive data can exacerbate worry. Limit your exposure and focus on uplifting content.
4. **Establish Routines**: Structure and routines can bring a sense of normalcy. Try to maintain regular habits, even simple ones like reading at a certain hour or nightly gratitude journaling.
5. **Engage in Relaxation Techniques**: Methods such as

progressive muscle relaxation or guided imagery can help shift from a state of worry to one of calm.

6. **Limit 'Worry Time'**: Designate a specific, brief period for worrying. Once that time is over, purposefully shift your attention.

7. **Seek Support**: Lean on trusted individuals who offer a listening ear, wise counsel, or even just comforting company.

8. **Physical Activity**: Engage in physical exercises to release pent-up tension and clear the mind.

9. **Listen to Uplifting Music**: Music can be a balm for the soul. Create a playlist of comforting or worship songs that redirect your focus to peace and trust.

The journey from worry to peace is a continuous one, demanding intentionality and consistent effort. Yet, it's also a rewarding voyage, offering a sanctuary of tranquility amidst life's tempests. By consciously deciding to turn from the path of worry and walk toward the realm of peace, guided by faith and trust, you're choosing a more fulfilling, balanced, and joyous life experience.

CONTENTMENT: THE HIDDEN Treasure

Paul wrote, *"I have learned to be content whatever the circumstances."* (Philippians 4:11) By diving into Paul's journey and other biblical narratives, you'll uncover the hidden treasure of contentment and how it serves as a shield against the darts of worry.

Contentment, often misunderstood as complacency or lack of ambition, is truly a serene satisfaction with the present moment, irrespective of its imperfections. It's a soul-deep realization that true joy isn't hinged on external circumstances but on an inner alignment and peace. The Apostle Paul writes in Philippians 4:11-12, *"I have learned to be content whatever the circumstances. I know what it is to be in need, and I know what it is to have plenty. I have learned the secret of being content in any and every situation."* This suggests that contentment is not passive acceptance but a cultivated skill

Perspective on Contentment:

Beyond Materialism: True contentment isn't about acquiring more but cherishing what one has, seeing the value and blessing in the present.

Inner vs. Outer World: While the outer world might be chaotic, contentment ensures the inner world remains tranquil and balanced.

The Antidote to Comparison: In an era of social media and constant comparison, contentment acts as a shield, protecting one from the pitfalls of envy and dissatisfaction.

Practical Checklist: Cultivating Contentment

1. **Gratitude Journal**: Daily jot down things you're grateful for. This practice shifts focus from what's lacking to what's abundant in life.
2. **Limit Social Media**: Reduce exposure to platforms that often spark comparison and feelings of inadequacy.
3. **Mindfulness Meditation**: Engage in practices that root you in the present moment, allowing you to appreciate the here and now.
4. **Celebrate Small Wins**: Recognize and celebrate minor achievements and simple joys instead of waiting for monumental milestones.
5. **Surround Yourself with Content Individuals**: Seek out individuals who radiate contentment and let their perspective influence and inspire you.
6. **Refrain from Retail Therapy**: Avoid the trap of believing purchasing items will bring lasting happiness. More often, it's a fleeting feeling.
7. **Serve Others**: Engage in acts of service. Helping others often shifts the focus from personal wants to the needs of others,

fostering gratitude and contentment.

8. **Read and Reflect**: Dive into scriptures, books, or articles that delve into the theme of contentment.

9. **Nature Walks**: Spend time in nature. The simplicity and beauty of the natural world often inspire feelings of contentment.

1. **Positive Affirmations**: Repeat affirmations that reinforce contentment, such as *"I am enough,"* or *"I cherish the present."*

2. **Seek Counseling**: If feelings of discontent are deep-rooted, consider therapy or counseling to address underlying issues.

Contentment, the hidden treasure, is attainable for everyone. Unlike fleeting happiness dependent on external factors, contentment is an inner reservoir of peace. When discovered and nurtured, it becomes a guiding force, ensuring that life, with its ebb and flow, is navigated with grace, gratitude, and an unwavering smile.

Your Role in the Larger Story

Finally, remember that you are part of a more magnificent narrative, God's grand story. By understanding your role and significance in this larger tale, the daily worries start to fade, replaced by a sense of purpose and divine mission.

Every individual, with their unique experiences, gifts, and challenges, plays a vital role in the tapestry of life. Often, in the chaos of daily life, this larger narrative is obscured. However, scriptures remind us time and again that everyone has a divine purpose. Jeremiah 29:11 asserts, *"For I know the plans I have for you," declares the LORD, "plans to prosper you and not to harm you, plans to give you hope and a future."* Thus, recognizing one's role in this larger narrative can provide clarity, purpose, and a deeper connection to the Divine.

Perspective on Your Role in the Larger Story:

Unique Yet Interconnected: Each individual's journey is distinct, but together they weave the grand narrative of life and God's plan.

Purpose Amidst Uncertainty: Even in times of doubt or confusion, there's a higher purpose guiding each step, even if it's not immediately evident.

The Ripple Effect: Every act, no matter how small, creates ripples in the universe, impacting others and the broader story in ways unimaginable.

Practical Checklist: Discovering Your Role in the Larger Story

1. **Reflect on Past Experiences**: Review personal milestones, both highs and lows. How have they shaped you and influenced others?

2. **Dive into Scriptures**: Engage with biblical characters and stories. How did they discern their roles in God's plan?
3. **Seek Spiritual Mentorship**: Connect with mentors or spiritual leaders who can provide guidance and share their own journeys.
4. **Journaling**: Maintain a regular journal. Documenting thoughts and experiences can offer insights into one's evolving role and purpose.
5. **Actively Listen**: Engage in deep conversations with loved ones. Sometimes, insights about our roles come from those who know us best.
6. **Prayer and Meditation**: Dedicate time to seek divine guidance, asking for clarity about your role in the larger narrative.
7. **Participate in Service**: Engaging in community service can provide insights into how one fits into and impacts the broader community and world.
8. **Attend Workshops/Retreats**: Participate in spiritual retreats or workshops focused on discovering purpose and understanding one's role in the grand scheme.
9. **Embrace New Opportunities**: Sometimes, stepping out of your comfort zone reveals unforeseen paths and purposes.
10. **Create a Vision Board**: Visualize your aspirations, goals, and how you perceive your role in the world.

1. **Stay Open and Flexible**: As life evolves, so might your role. Stay open to changes, understanding that the larger story is dynamic.

Recognizing one's role in the larger story is a lifelong journey of discovery, filled with moments of clarity and periods of questioning. Yet, the pursuit of this understanding is in itself a beautiful endeavor, leading to a life lived with purpose, passion, and a profound connection to the Divine and to the intricate web of life and humanity.

Exhaustive Checklist: Transitioning from Worry to Peace and Contentment

1. **Self-awareness and Reflection**
   - Identify specific worries.
   - Reflect on their origins.
   - Acknowledge your feelings without judgment.
2. **Scriptural Engagement**
   - Meditate on scriptures emphasizing peace (e.g., Philippians 4:6-7).
   - Dive deep into biblical stories of trust amidst uncertainty.
3. **Prayer and Spiritual Connection**
   - Dedicate time daily to communicate with God.
   - Surrender your worries through prayer.
   - Seek divine guidance and strength.

1. **Mindfulness and Meditation**
   - Engage in deep breathing exercises.
   - Practice grounding techniques.
   - Embrace the present moment without fixating on past or future.
2. **Journaling and Expression**
   - Pen down feelings, worries, and reflections.
   - Track moments of gratitude daily.
   - Note instances where worry was overcome by peace.
3. **Positive Affirmations**
   - Craft personalized affirmations to combat worry.
   - Repeat affirmations during moments of anxiety.

1. **Limit Exposure to Stressors**
   - Limit news and social media intake.

- ○ Filter out negative influences, both online and offline.

2. **Healthy Lifestyle Choices**
   - ○ Adopt a balanced diet.
   - ○ Ensure adequate sleep.
   - ○ Engage in regular physical activity.

3. **Connect with Supportive Individuals**
   - ○ Share worries and seek advice from trusted family or friends.
   - ○ Consider joining support groups or faith communities.

4. **Limit 'Worry Time'**

- Designate specific periods to address worries, then move on.

1. **Seek Professional Guidance**

- Consider therapy or counseling.
- Engage in workshops focusing on stress management and emotional well-being.

1. **Engage in Acts of Kindness**

- Volunteer.
- Assist others in need.
- Perform random acts of kindness to shift focus outward.

1. **Nature Engagement**

- Spend time outdoors.
- Practice grounding exercises in natural surroundings.

1. **Art and Creative Outlets**

- Engage in art, music, writing, or other creative pursuits to express and process emotions.

1. **Educate Yourself**

- Read books or articles on managing worry.
- Attend seminars or webinars about cultivating peace and contentment.

1. **Visualization Techniques**

- Imagine scenarios where you react to challenges with peace.
- Visualize a worry-free version of yourself.

1. **Develop Routines**

- Cultivate daily routines for stability.
- Integrate relaxation and self-care routines.

1. **Embrace Change**

- Accept that change is a part of life.
- Focus on elements you can control.

1. **Foster a Gratitude Mindset**

- Identify daily blessings.
- Maintain a gratitude journal.

1. **Establish Boundaries**

- Learn to say 'no' when necessary.
- Prioritize tasks and responsibilities.

1. **Celebrate Progress**

- Recognize and celebrate moments of peace and contentment.
- Reward yourself for milestones achieved in your journey.

Shifting from worry to peace and contentment is a multifaceted journey. This exhaustive checklist provides comprehensive steps that, when embraced, can foster a transformation in mindset, enabling individuals to navigate life with serenity and joy.

Conclusion

Worry has been humanity's age-old companion. Yet, as you've journeyed through these pages, the scriptures shine a light on a path paved with trust, surrender, and contentment. As you embark on this transformative journey, may the chains of worry shatter, replaced by the liberating wings of faith. Remember, in the grand tapestry of life, God is the master weaver, turning every thread, every worry, into a masterpiece of His design.

Don't miss out!

Visit the website below and you can sign up to receive emails whenever Minister Jeremy B. Sims publishes a new book. There's no charge and no obligation.

https://books2read.com/r/B-A-AHMAB-HMFOC

BOOKS2READ

Connecting independent readers to independent writers.

Did you love *Why Worrying is A Waste: A Biblical Perspective*? Then you should read *So You've Been Baptized, What's Next: The Road to Discipleship*[1] by Minister Jeremy B. Sims!

[2]

THis book will inspire you to embark on a transformative journey to understand what it truly means to be a disciple of Christ. Through the exploration of faith, scripture, service, and community, this book provides guidance and inspiration for those seeking to deepen their spiritual commitment and live a life dedicated to the teachings of Jesus. It serves as a roadmap for the ongoing process of discipleship, helping individuals find purpose, meaning, and fulfillment in their faith journey

---

1. https://books2read.com/u/4Xel65

2. https://books2read.com/u/4Xel65

Also by Minister Jeremy B. Sims

Stop Blaming the Adversary: It's You!
From Milk to Meat: The Journey of Spiritual Maturity
So You've Been Baptized, What's Next: The Road to Discipleship
Why Worrying is A Waste: A Biblical Perspective